I See You... You Cannot Hide!

Dr. Dyoni Cole

I See You ... You Cannot Hide!
Dyoni, Inc.
Info@dyonicole.com

Cover Design by: Dr. Dyoni Cole
ISBN-13: 978-153704298
ISBN-10: 1537304291
Copyright © by Dr. Dyoni Cole
Editor: Janet Devlin

Unless otherwise noted, all Scripture quotations
are from the New International Version (NIV) of the
Bible.

Printed in the United States of America
Frist Printing: August 2016

To order additional copies please contact:
Dyoni, Inc. Website: www.dyonicole.com

Foreword

This is an outstanding project from Dr. Dyoni Cole, my sister, friend, and co-laborer in The Lord's Vineyard. Dr. Dyoni's gracious, transparent, and "tell it like it is" style presented a sensitive topic in an authentically candid manner while balanced with wisdom, personal experience, and the Word of God. All of this gives the project credence and integrity, qualifying it as a must-read not only for believers but unbelievers as well.

She brought the light of truth to a hidden, dark, subtle, yet prevalent spirit in our society and even in our houses of worship that remains unaddressed. A spirit that we've learned to hide behind with our expensive suits, wonderful weaves, wigs, and hats. Behind the perfect MAC makeup, powder, eyeshadows, and lipsticks. Behind the Louis Vuitton heels and purses. Behind the fixed smiles, education, and the constant, rehearsed postures of one who is indelibly composed and put together. Yet, underneath it all, remains a real person with feelings and emotions that have been violated, bruised, and wounded by *The Spirit of Deception.*

Deception has many faces and expressions, but I strongly believe that "self-deception" is the worst deception, which causes one to live in denial of reality that exists and yet refuses to accept. This denial and refusal of acceptance becomes the playing field of the enemy who exploits and takes full advantage of the vulnerable and susceptible person through manipulation.

I See You... You Cannot Hide!

Purely and only by the Grace of God, as in His divine influence and enablement, Dr. Dyoni takes us through her journey of pain and disappointment—emotional, mental, psychological, and physical trauma as a result of this diabolical spirit, hence the title of her book, "I See You ... You Cannot Hide!" This expose takes us behind the scenes of God's Chosen Vessel—Dr. Dyoni's story of rejection, abandonment, betrayal, and shame. However, she also shares her process of acknowledging and coming to terms with truth, and finally, by the Grace of God, found healing, liberty, and emancipation through Christ. She showed that as part of "Generation Next" as "Millennial" there are very real challenges of navigating and maneuvering our perverted societal arena, and yet one can still be able to come out victorious and more than a conqueror.

Dr. Dyoni Cole

The redemptive essence of Dr. Dyoni's intriguing memoir is, when God has a plan for your life, He will always awaken you as He did with Jacob in Genesis 28, "And Jacob awoke and said, the Lord is in this place, but I knew it not." God awakens us and brings us to a conscious awareness that through it all, He was always with us.

Dr. Dyoni, I truly salute you in this amazing expose that I know will be a tool and handbook for true healing and deliverance to a generation and generations to come.

Pastor Sarah Morgan
Vision International Ministries
Los Angeles, CA

Dedication

I dedicate this book back to the Lord, for it was through him, I was able to complete this assignment. I also dedicate this book to every individual who is going through a situation that seems unbearable. As God was faithful in my situation, I am confident he will be faithful in your situation as well. His plan for you is of good and not of evil. Trust him as you go through your process.

Forgiveness ... Deliverance ... Freedom ...
~XOXOXOX Dr. Dyoni

Dr. Dyoni Cole

Table of Contents

Introduction

Sometimes we cover up our truth by muting our voice to protect the feelings and heart of those we love at the expense of allowing others to go through situations where our truth could help set them free. Understand it is not about making others look bad or attempting to throw anyone under the bus, but rather it's about helping others in the very area God used to develop our character and also graced us to conquer.

Sharing this life-changing situation was not an easy one because I was forced to come to grips with all aspects of my truth. As I wrote, I was forced to re-live the situation and honestly, some aspect of the situation made me sick to my stomach. But, my desire to uncover and share my truth with you outweighed it all. I hope the transparency of my truth will enable you to look at your situation from a different perspective. It may appear to be one thing, but if you look deeper, you will see it is something completely different.

Disclosure: This book is about me, Dr. Dyoni D. Cole, and only me. I wrote this to expose my truth in every aspect ... nothing more and nothing less.

CHAPTER ONE
Transition

Transition is never easy; it requires time, lots of patience, and support. In my case, transition is a process that requires me to go through series of steps before I am fully able to adjust and find a flow for the new chapter of my journey. Although I have endured numerous transitions, this last transition almost cost me my life.

It began in 2008 when I made the decision to enroll in a doctoral program. I had no idea what was in store for me, but I stepped out in faith and started an unimaginable journey. As a full-time online student, I continued to work as a full-time receptionist at a private gym, taught dance classes with a production company part-time, and faithfully served in ministry. My days started at 4 am and ended around 12 am most days. My life was hectic: ministry, school, work. There was no time for extra activities—or should I say fun. This was my life at the time, and I accepted it. I put my all into everything I was responsible for and made the best of my situation.

As I completed my coursework and passed my comp exam, I prepared for the dissertation process with excitement. Not knowing what was coming ahead, I continued my heavy load of ministry, work, and school until I was forced to make a decision to decrease my time serving in ministry. It was a difficult decision because the four walls of the church became a home away from home.

Decreasing my time in ministry enabled me to spend the time needed to focus on completing my dissertation. It was hard because I felt obligated to be inside those four walls. I felt guilty for not being there and standing on my post, doing my duties within the church. Many times, I wanted to renege on my decision and go back to the hectic schedule that kept me always on the go. Eventually, I had thoughts of completely removing myself from ministry to focus on school. This part of my transition was hard because I felt numerous emotions. I was confused and angry at the same time. With so many different emotions going on within me, I held on until I was forced to make yet another decision that was drastic. I had to entirely quit my time in ministry and solely focus on school. It was difficult, but I knew it was something that needed to happen. The feeling I felt when I had to make the decision was horrifying. Within months, I completed my dissertation and prepared for graduation. I knew one day I would reach the finish line, but it seemed so unlikely to happen due to the many unforeseen circumstances.

Graduation Day

On the day of graduation, I was in a new place of hope. I wondered what was next for me. Not knowing what would present itself in this next chapter of my journey, I was surrounded by those who loved me, and I was thankful in so many ways. The day was amazing. But, additional events made the day even better. I was offered a position in a small consulting firm by an organization I respected in so many ways. In awe, I needed some time to process the invitation because, with this new position, many changes would have to take place in my life. I tried not to give thought to it at the time because I wanted to enjoy my graduation day.

A few days went by, and I made a few calls to get additional information on this new position. It was the perfect position being that I was a recent graduate. It was ideal, provided great promise, and was almost too hard to believe. After a few additional days, I agreed to take the position. I prepared my two weeks' notice and mentally gathered myself for yet another shift in my transition. My life was changing, and I welcomed the change. I thought the hard part was over; I finished my dissertation, successfully defended my dissertation, graduated, and landed a new position. Things appeared to fall into place. All I had to do was continue to trust God and allow him to lead the way.

New Job

My last day as a receptionist was hard. I was ready to move on, but I had no idea that leaving would be so difficult. I met some wonderful people I grew to love and care about. Leaving was bittersweet, but I knew I had to go in order to transition into the next chapter of my life.

I was so excited to start my new position. The first day was like the first day of school. I had no idea what to expect, but I was open to learning and experiencing new things. I was surrounded by new people and a culture that I was not familiar with, but I welcomed it with open arms. In some ways, the environment reminded me of the ministry I once faithfully served in, so I was taken aback just a little. Everyone was very friendly and welcomed me into their environment. During my time of training, I learned about the company's policies, procedures, and culture. It was interesting, and I was eager for the opportunity.

Within the first month, I received my first, second, and third client. It was a little difficult at first because I had yet to find a good flow. I was only going by how I was taught, but I had not made it my own and was very uncomfortable. Once I found my flow, I began to get comfortable and found myself getting more clients. Things were looking good. However, there were a few things that bothered me, but I decided not to address them because they were personal pet peeves of mine. I turned my head because the bigger picture was assisting my clients to success. Although I made the decision not to address the issue, other things began to surface, but I still decided to remain silent. I remained silent because the organization had plans to relocate, so I figured the relocation would solve the issues I had. Nevertheless, I focused on my clients and continued to work on my projects.

Once I mastered my flow, I began to get projects out. It was so incredible to mentor and coach individuals to complete their dissertation projects successfully. As I completed one project, I would get two, maybe three, new clients. I was moving pretty quickly, but I loved it because it kept me on my toes. There was never a dull minute in my eight-hour day in the office.

Nevertheless, I enjoyed my time away from the office. I would spend my lunch at a nearby park to process and calm down. I would take walks and even do short runs to decrease the stress that would try to come upon me while in the office. When I looked up, I had over twenty active clients. It became totally hectic, but

I was used to a hectic schedule, and I welcomed it. I took pride in giving of myself to help others reach their goal; it was my passion. Things were moving well, my clients were focused, and I was getting things done. However, I began to get too involved in my work because I began to feel the weight of a few of my clients. I knew the stress they felt, I found myself feeling the weight of their stress, and I began to get stressed out.

This new position was a blessing and seemed to be too good to be true at first, but after six months, it began to feel like a burden. I began to think about everything I went through in ministry and with work I became annoyed, angry, and frustrated. It was a bad time for me. During this time, my sister introduced me to a young man named Levi. Levi had questions concerning natural hair care, and although I was incredibly busy, I made an effort to assist him with his questions. We actually scheduled a time to meet for a hair care consultation. After all, I needed an outlet for the stress I felt from my job, so taking the time to discuss hair was a perfect outlet for me.

Never apologize for being who you are. You are fearfully and wonderfully made (Psalm 139:14).

Chapter Two
Blindsided

We met at Levi's apartment, discussed his hair care, and I provided some advice on how he could take better care of his dreadlocks. Overall, the appointment went well. We talked about many things. He shared some personal things with me, which was a little odd being it was our first encounter. He said I was easy to talk to, and he felt comfortable talking with me. It was a rather deep conversation. It was odd because everything about him was different—the way he spoke, the way he carried himself—his very demeanor was different. In the midst of our conversation, the front door opened, and a guy walked in. He was a friend, and I assumed it was his roommate. Anyhow, we concluded our discussion and he walked me to my car, and I drove off.

Months went by, and Levi contacted me again. At this time, it was quite established that I was his natural hair care consultant as I was helping him with his hair. We scheduled a time to meet at his apartment on a Friday night. Once I concluded the duties at my job, I traveled to his apartment, parked, called him, and told him I was outside. When he came down to get me, he gave me a hug that was different and actually caught me off guard. In the midst of the hug, he told me his mom was in the apartment. I thought it was weird, but I figured I was just doing this guy's hair and nothing more so I let it go.

Anyhow, we went upstairs, and part of me wondered if it was a setup—that his mom was at the apartment. But, he and I only had a business relationship, nothing more than that, so again, I brushed it off. When I entered the apartment, he introduced me to his mom, and she seemed to be quite a friendly lady. We had an awesome conversation, but I realized that she treated Levi like a child. It was so familiar ... it reminded me of how my grandmother treated my dad. Once I finished with his hair maintenance, he walked me downstairs, gave me a hug, and said thank you.

A few days went by, and I had a quick thought about Levi. I ended up texting him to check on the status of his hair. He texted back and said that his hair was perfect, and he really loved it. I texted back by sending a picture of myself with the word "wonderful!" A day or two later, I heard from a few friends of mine that he constantly asked about me. I joked around with the thought that this young guy wanted to holler, but was afraid to step to me. As I laughed it off and went about my business, he eventually texted me, and we talked. I had to admit, it was nice to have a man text me to see how I was doing. From there, we began to text frequently. I did not think much of it because he was younger and had nothing to offer me, so I did not take it very seriously. Nevertheless, I continued to entertain it. One day he asked me out, and I said yes. I was thrilled because it had been a long time since I'd gone out on a date. It had been over seven years since I had some kind of connection with a man, so I was looking forward to it. The way he asked me was so different. He was such a square, but I liked it because he was something different ... something I was not used to.

Know your issues ... be in tune with your issues, but never underestimate them because they will blow up in your face.

Chapter Three
Indwelling Sin

He was smart, and unlike any man I had ever communicated with. I remember talking about the date with a friend, and she was not happy about it because I told her I was not interested in him, but here I was planning a date with him. Anyhow, we planned the date, and I was excited. We made plans to go to the movies on a Tuesday night, and he asked that I be on time. I got dressed, and I have to say, I was pretty cute!

I arrived at the theater only to realize he was not there. He was very late! I was upset and almost started to leave, or see the movie myself, but I waited for him. When he arrived, he called, and I answered. He asked some questions, and I

17

provided the answers. After he had parked, he walked up to the ticket counter. I sat in my car and watched him for a minute or two. I exited my car and greeted him at the ticket counter. It was obvious that the movie had already started; of course, I acted as if I was upset and made sure he knew it. He asked if I was hungry and I said not really, but we could get something to eat. He said, "Follow me." We got into our cars and pulled off.

We drove until we stopped at a nearby restaurant. Strange thing, he wanted to sit at the bar, but not me. I found a seat at a booth. We sat, we talked, and we eventually ordered some food. I ordered a veggie pizza with a glass of wine. He ordered a small salad and a glass of beer. I was surprised that he was making conversation. He was exceptionally intelligent, and I enjoyed our talk. He shared with me about his family. He also shared a little of his background, and I shared mine with him. I was straightforward with him concerning my past. He was shocked at some of the things I shared. I told him that I was a pretty open and honest person. I can be off the hook at times, so I like to ... in my own little way ... warn people. I told him, "I've been hurt before, and I believe in being open and honest with people. You know, allow people to know who you are and provide them the opportunity to decide whether they want to deal with you or not." I was totally candid with him— maybe too honest—but that was me being me.

Overall, it was a pretty cool first date considering how it started. We sat and talked for a long time and decided to leave around midnight. We walked outside, and it felt so strange to me because Levi was unlike anyone I had ever gone out with, and I wanted to know more about him.

We started to talk more and more on the phone. It seemed like everything was moving so quickly. The entire time, my friend was against me talking to him and seeing him. She wanted me to cut him off, but I could not. I started being secretive, not sharing any information with anyone, and I began to spend more time with him. Levi had such potential, and I saw the greatness in him, although he had difficulty seeing it for himself. I enjoyed hanging out with him. He made me smile, provided comfort for me, I was able to be myself with him, and he was funny in his own way. He also had a mystery about him that drove me crazy. I wanted to know more about him—about his past. He was different, and I needed different in my life. I had an idea what I was dealing with, but it was a little confusing because he would open up to me, but then turn around and be distant.

The Plot

One day, Levi needed to speak with me and invited me over. He shared with me why he was so distant and felt like he was not in a good place to be with me. He asked me what I wanted from him, and I told him his friendship ... to be a close friend. I only expected him to be honest and open with me. I just wanted him, and to spend time with him. Yes, he had a lot of issues that needed to be worked out, but I was willing to deal with them. I was willing to show him that he was worthy of love. He was worthy of the best and I was the best. My love came with no conditions. We had our first real kiss that night, and it was incredible! He held me with confidence; I liked it, and I melted in his arms.

A shift occurred after that moment, and we began to see each other in the mornings. I would go over to Levis' apartment after my early morning workouts, and we would talk and make out. I felt like I was in high school again ... a schoolgirl again. I could be myself and have fun. That was one of the things I loved about him. He allowed me to be me.

We did struggle with the temptation of sex, and we would be all over each other. We practically would have sex with our clothes on. We were doing too much too soon. If it went too far, I would stop it, or he would stop it. I shared with him that I was celibate and wanted to wait to have sex until marriage. He seemed quite cool about it. Actually, he too was celibate. He said he was worth more than sex, so he stopped having sex. I thought his response was fascinating, but I knew there was more to it.

A week or so went by, and we ended up doing a little too much and going a little too far. We were moving fast, and things became intense. With everything going on, I knew I needed to leave him alone. Deep inside, I knew he was wrong for me because I often found myself in compromising situations and that was a clear sign that I needed to step back. The red flags would appear often, and I would talk to him about them. I would tell him frequently that I needed to release him, but I had such a hard time doing it. Maybe it was me being selfish and wanting to keep him to myself. A part of me knew he had a huge heart, and once he opened up to me, I would be the recipient of the love that was within his heart.

We actually had a conversation in which he told me he could not give me what I needed. He told me he was in a place of transition. He gave details, and I thought this was a positive thing because he had trust issues, but he trusted me enough to share his flaws with me. I wanted to go deep with him. I wanted to touch his flaws because it was those flaws that made him the person he was. I saw his potential, and I wanted him to see it too. I needed him to understand that, in spite of his past, he was worthy of love.

Do not settle ... you are worth so much more.

Chapter Four
Self-Inflicted Inward Battle

Once I shared some information with a close friend, she was not happy about it. In the last relationship I had, I got hurt pretty badly, and I put in place some really strict boundaries. Boundaries such as no one-on-one dates—only group gatherings. No hugging, kissing, or holding hands, and, no receiving calls after 10:30 pm. All the boundaries I put in place went out the door! I never paid attention that I dismantled my very own boundaries and the standards I put in place. When I was confronted about this, I gave some lame excuses. Red flags were all over the place, but I continued seeing and talking to Levi.

No one liked Levi because I became a different person—and it was not a better person. Everyone wanted me to end all communication with him completely, but I was torn. I knew I needed to, but did not want to. The more my friends told me to leave him alone, the more I gravitated to him. I guess I could not see what was really going on because I was blindsided, yet knew what I was doing was wrong and tried to justify my actions. I found myself defending him and saying things like, "You just don't know him. He is a really nice guy and is very smart, with such potential." I failed to realize I had lowered my standards for him.

I also failed to realize that he completely disrespected a friend of mine, the person who introduced us. When it was brought to my attention, I confronted him, but I still did not end it. Instead, I tried to slowly decrease our time together to eventually let him go, but I understood the issues he had. Like me, he'd been hurt too, and I was sensitive to that; I did not want to add to his pain. I tried to handle him with kid gloves, as I did not want to cause him any harm. He opened up to me and trusted me. Not wanting to hurt him, I made excuses to stay and found myself deeper and deeper in a situation that I knew I needed to walk away from.

Mental Battles

All the while, I went through mental battles in my mind because I knew I needed to release him. My character and integrity was tested, but I was in so deep— I could not. All I knew was that my attention was removed from my stressful job, and I was spending time with Levi, who had such promise. I tried to let go on many occasions, and we went back and forth. I always reneged on it because we kissed, he comforted me, and I shared a special connection with him. There was a connection I never had with any man before him, and I was mesmerized. I remember asking him, what did you do to me? Why do I care about you so much?

I was clearly gone. I saw him in his future and what I saw was wonderful. I saw the greatness in him, and I actually fell in love with it ... his potential. We would spend more time with each other, and I would hide the fact that I fell in love with him because I knew no one approved of him. My household began to be disrupted. My relationships with family and friends were on the rocks, and I knew it, but I still just could not walk away. There was a major stronghold on me, and its name was Levi. What was the deal with me? I just met this person, and I was all over the place. My emotions were so strong regarding him. I found myself in tears because I knew I needed to give him up. Yet, I found myself drawing closer to him and spending more time with him instead of disconnecting from him. I was so confused because he had nothing to offer me, but he had such an intense hold on me. I knew there were other men with so much more to offer, yet I picked this guy. Things were moving so quickly, and I allowed it. I felt and saw all the warnings, but I was weak, stressed out, and I did not have much fight left in me. I obviously was not myself, and I continued to justify and make excuses for all of my actions.

Cover Up

Every morning I sat in my car crying. I wanted to share what I felt, but I did not want to hurt or disappoint anyone. I wanted to please my family, friends, Levi, and myself all at the same time. I almost killed myself trying to please everyone. I did not want to expose what I was doing because I knew I had no business being with Levi. I was in complete disobedience because I knew I needed to let him go, but I was so weak. God was tugging at my heart, but I did not want to take heed, so I did numerous things to hide. It was time for me to come to grips with my issues—

everything was blowing up in my face and was being exposed. I could not hide any longer. My character issues, my issues with how I dealt with men, my issues dealing with my self-worth and self-esteem, and my issues with ministry, but I did not want to face them, and I found myself deeper in a situation as I continued to run from them. I ran from God and doing that which I knew he was calling me to do.

I tried to reach out for help, but help was nowhere to be found. At least not the help I was looking for. I was struggling and struggling badly, but my pride would not let me admit that I was in a life or death situation. Levi was my drug, and I was addicted. I was in a trance, and I wanted to go in deep with him. We discussed marriage, children, and I was all for it. I was ready for a family—at least I thought I was. I was so unstable in my emotions; one minute I was up and the next minute I was in tears. *What the heck was going on with me?* It was a war going on inside of me, and I was losing fast. I had separated from my accountability, so I was out there trying to find my way. This was outrageous! *How did I allow everything to get this way?* This situation I was in was self-inflicted; I did it to myself ... it was suicidal. Had I just taken heed to the red flags I'd seen early on. Had I just been obedient, had a little more fight inside of me, just maybe I could have fought harder, stood strong, and resisted. The peculiar thing was that God always provided a way of escape, but somehow I always found myself back in Levi's arms. I just could not stay away. I began to dislike myself. I hated what I was doing, but I still did not want to hurt him. Why was I like this? I was in tears all the time, I was no longer happy, but honestly—I never was happy.

Yes, indeed, I did this to myself. I became someone I did not even recognize. It was as if I lived a double life. It was taking a toll on me and every aspect of my life. Again, I knew I needed to let go—to release him, but for some reason I just could not. I wanted to protect him— protect his heart ... I just did not want to harm him. I knew the hurt he suffered and the state he was in, so I felt I would betray him and make it worse if I walked away from him. I cared deeply about him. I wanted and needed him to understand that my actions aligned with my words.

Sometimes you have to close your eyes, endure the turbulence, and trust God to pull you through. HANG IN THERE!

Chapter Five
Set-Up

Things were out of control. I was so
unstable, and it was a wild sight. I
struggled with the thought of really letting
Levi go because I was hurting so much
inside. Within this time, he mentioned he
was relocating to a different state.
Although this was a good thing, it hurt
because I was faced with knowing that I
should have had the strength to release
him on my own. But, God, with His many
attempts, clearly wanted this person out of
my life. With this new information of him
moving, I finally built up the strength to
let Levi go. At least, I built up the courage
to release him with words from my mouth.
I mean, I had to ... he was leaving, and I
figured once he moved, everything would

just die down and fizzle out. So, why not start the process of letting go ...

During my time apart from him, I was able to see some of my own personal issues, repent, and see what direction I needed to go in. I finally made the decision to not run from my call of ministry. I decided to accept the call to get licensed as a minister. However, there were so many reasons why I did not want to get licensed as a minister: I would be held at a higher level of accountability and would feel the pressure of perfection. I grew up in ministry and saw so much. I saw things most people would never imagine could be done in ministry. I was hurt so many times by individuals in leadership positions (pastors and ministers) in the church, and I did not want to connect myself to that. There was so much that was attached to me running, to me not wanting to be enlisted in the community of ministers.

In any event, I had an opportunity to talk out my issues with a close friend and came to grips with one major issue. I realized I was full of anger, hurt, and I hated what I had endured in ministry. I hated what I saw, the people that hurt me and those who sat back and watched it all happen and did nothing. It made so much sense why I struggled to move forward in what God wanted for my life. In the midst of my revelation, I began to think about Levi as now what I understood to be a distraction. How I placed myself in a situation that I knew, I had no business being in. The emotions and thoughts were so heavy, and on the sixth day of me releasing him, I called him and asked if we could talk. He agreed, and I drove over to his apartment.

Once I arrived, he met me outside, and we embraced. We began to talk, and he comforted me, told me that he loved me, and was willing to do whatever I wanted and needed him to do for us to be together. I shared with him that I finally decided to stop running and had accepted my call to be licensed as a minister. He was glad about my decision and told me that he was happy for me.

His Departure

A few days went by and it was time for Levi to move. Although I knew I needed to move forward, in my heart I still had a difficult time letting go. I still wanted to be with him, and he wanted to be with me. He wrote a poem and presented it to me the day he left. It was a beautiful poem and it made me feel so special.

Later that night, I was checking my social media sites, and I came across Levi's social media site. It was so cool because it displayed a few of his poems. I was eager to read more of his writing and to my surprise; the same poem he gave me was on his site. It was a poem that he had written exactly two years prior. The poem he gave me was supposed to be something inspired by me; the hurt I felt was indescribable. I called him, and he confessed and made some lame excuse. He allowed me to believe that he had written the poem for me. In this, I began to question everything concerning us. If someone could be deceptive about writing a poem, what else was he deceptive about? The foolish thing was, it was still not enough for me to walk away, I still tried to work things out—me—not him. I genuinely cared for him and loved him and could not understand why he was deceptive and deceptive for no reason. He contributed nothing, and it was becoming obvious. Yet, we continued to talk every day. We were getting closer, and I became more delusional. I really believed I had a future with him, at least I really wanted one with him, and I went out of my way to show him that I was serious.

Fighting

A few weeks went by, and I decided to go on a special consecration. I needed to fast and go into much prayer being that my licensing ceremony was a month and a few weeks away. I spoke with Levi and shared with him that I was going on this consecration, which required me to separate myself from him for a month. He was a little confused, but once I explained my need to step back, he understood and was okay. I figured this would be the turning point of everything, and I was finally in a place to obey and receive what was in store for me. I was excited and scared all at the same time because I did not know what to expect.

The night before my consecration, I spoke with Levi all night long. I loved talking with him and knew I was not going to be able to for a while, so I tried to keep him on the phone until midnight. Twenty minutes until midnight, I shared some really personal things with him, and he shared some personal things with me. Right before midnight, we hung up, and the consecration was in full effect. I was sure I would hear from God and have the strength to do what was needed in every aspect of my life ... but little did I know what headed my way.

I See You... You Cannot Hide!

The pain you feel has a predestined purpose in your life ... acknowledge the pain ... touch the pain ... feel the pain ... accept the pain ... grow from the pain.

Chapter Six
Brokenness

In week one, I spent most of my time in prayer, worship, and reading the Bible. During that time, when I was not in prayer or reading the Bible, my mind would revisit different conversations I had with Levi and questions would arise because something just did not add up. I realized he said some things that were contradictive, but I did not catch it at the time. The more I revisited our conversations, the more questions I began to have. I also began to have mental battles, whereas I began to be tormented in my mind. My mind was playing tricks on me. I began to feel he was going to find someone else during my time away from him. The mind games got so bad that, at the beginning of the second week, I called him and spoke with him for fifteen minutes. I asked a few questions, and he provided answers. He mentioned to me that he feared I would one day find someone who would give me what I needed, wanted, and deserved right now. This was a constant fear he had. I thought it to be interesting, and I made the comment, "Why would you want to be in something where you feel so insecure?" I told him I did not want him to worry or fear this and tried to console him. I asked him whether he was sure about me. Somehow, he turned it around and made me feel like I was wrong for asking such questions. He said he knew I was changing my mind about our relationship and that he was right all along. I felt bad and assured him I was not changing my mind. If anything, my consecration would allow me to truly know how to move forward with him. Once we got on the same page, we ended the conversation, and I felt better. The mind games and torment ended for a brief moment, but after a day or two, they began again.

Mind Games

Battling with mind games, and the withdrawals of not speaking with Levi, I spent more time in prayer and worship. I began to pray for him and ask God to touch him. I began to feel enormously insecure and unsure of myself. I started wondering about why he would want to be in a relationship with me in the first place. I began to feel horribly inadequate and the games began to get worse. My heart would hurt; I felt this sharp pain in my chest, and I could not understand what it was. While all these things were going on, I began to feel sick, as if I had the flu. Again, when the fire was turned up, I got weak and called him, but this time, he did not answer. I must have called over twenty times! Eventually, I stopped, but I was a little upset that he did not answer.

The next morning, he texted me and told me that God told him that we could not talk again until I finished my consecration. He said he missed me, he loved me, and he could not wait until we could connect again. I told him that it ended in two weeks, and we would speak then. As I sent that text, my phone rang, and it was Levi. He shared with me what was going on with him and that he did not answer my call the day before because he was in meditation the entire day. He said that he was able to hear God clearly, and he wanted to be obedient. I was shocked and at a loss for words because this was a person who was distanced from God, but appeared to be working on his relationship. I was happy to hear this from him and told him I was glad we met and that I loved him. As I cried, I told him that I would connect with him in a few days, and we ended our conversation.

I continued to have mental battles— I felt insecure, weak, powerless, and unsure of myself in all things. I began to spend all my time praying against these things and asking God to help me. I needed the mind games to stop. They were torture, and the pain in my heart was unbearable. It felt like someone took a dagger and stabbed me in my heart. It hurt that badly.

Two days before my consecration was over, I remembered having so many questions. Instead of calling him, I wrote my questions and thoughts down:

> *I have so many questions. Do I still have your heart? Do you still want to spend the rest of your life with me? Am I still the*

one for you? I should be, but I am not too sure how your process went. It's been two weeks and two days, and I wonder what has changed? Has anything changed? The last time we spoke, you said you were madly in love with me ... has that changed? Are we still a "we"? Can we move forward and begin our chapter together as a couple? There are so many questions. I've gone through so many changes, but the way I feel about you has not changed. If anything, I am even more confident that I want you and I want to go deep with you— share your scars, feel your wounds, and love your heart. It has been a difficult month for me and honestly, I wished you could have been by my side helping me go through this, but I needed to deal with some things. I know through this month I showed you some crazy sides of me ... not too sure if you understand what I was going through. Again, do I still have your heart? Do you still want to spend the rest of your life with me? Do you still want me to have your babies? I still want those things. Are we going forward? Yes, there are so many things we need to discuss. Yes, we have to remain pure. Yes, there is little room for error ... Where do we stand exactly? Will we pick up where we left off? My heart hurts ... just wanting to speak

to you and get this over with ...
Our Talk.

Disobedience

However, during prayer on the last night of my consecration, it was clear that I needed to let Levi go. I knew God wanted my undivided attention, and he needed me to release him. Levi was a distraction; he was a distraction from the beginning, but I could not see it because I was so caught up in what I wanted. I went through so much torment and heartache that I was in a place to finally obey and get it done, but I needed a way to do it. Still being considerate about his wellbeing, I planned to break it to him slowly. I believed things would settle down because of my busy schedule as well as his. I was ready to speak with him; I was ready for our conversation.

The last day of my consecration seemed like a century. I so wanted to get it over with ... the conversation that was long overdue. I prayed to God and asked that He would have his way in the conversation and that I would not allow my emotions to take over as I had allowed so many times in the past. But when time came for me to call him, he answered, and a smile came upon my face. We shared a few words, and I told him that I needed to know if anything changed in regards to how he felt about me. He said no, but rather his feelings for me were stronger. I had some really tough questions for him that night, and he provided answers although they were not very solid. We made plans to talk later in the day, and I looked forward to it.

Later that afternoon we spoke and everything seemed okay. I told him I really appreciated how he allowed me to have my time and did not fight me on it. I asked him if he needed anything from me. He said he did not know what he needed, but he knew what he wanted. He wanted for us to speak in the morning so we could pray and to speak at night and pray before bed. I said I would be willing to try it out. We scheduled times whereas I would call him in the morning at a specific time and he would call me at night at a specific time. We agreed that we would start that night. We ended our conversation, and I went about my business.

Our scheduled time was approaching, so I made sure to be ready when he called. I waited for him and no call. Finally, I called him, and he said that he was just getting ready to call me. I was a little upset and addressed it. Once I finished addressing the issue we discussed our day, we prayed, and we ended our conversation. The next morning, I roused and did my usual routine, but this time, I got up a little earlier so I could call him at our scheduled time. I called him, he answered, and we prayed. Before we ended the conversation, he told me that he would call me on his way to work, I said okay and went about my business.

As I was driving to work, he called, and we spoke briefly. Everything seemed to be fine, but I noticed that he began to repeat a lot of things that I would say as if they were *his* words. He was mocking me and actually made me feel extremely little; I felt stupid. I began to feel insecure about everything, and my heart began to hurt like crazy.

Later that night, I prepared myself for his call. Although I was very busy, I wanted to keep my word and be available when he called, but he never called. Again, he displayed a lack of consideration for my time, and I was angry. I called him a few times, and he did not answer. Eventually, he texted me and told me that he was at a comic book store and would call me once he got home. I was not sure how I felt about that. Hours went by and still no call from him. By this time, I began to get worried, so I called him again and—no answer. I called yet again, and he answered and acted as if nothing was wrong, which angered me more! I asked if he was okay and he said yes. I told him I was worried that something had happened being that he failed to keep his commitment. We talked, and the conversation was horrible. We had nothing much to talk about. Finally, I said, "This is not going to work" and he replied, "Yes you're right, this is not going to work." I paused incredulous and said, "Are you serious?" Then, I went off on him. He began to say he needed to release me. I could not believe it! I knew that it would come to this, but there was so much attached to what he was doing. He set it up so well, made me feel so little, and then threw me to the side. I could not believe this was happening. My heart was broken, and I was in tears. He said some things that really hurt, but what hurt the most was how he handled the situation. The entire time I protected his feelings, and when he needed to protect my feelings, he failed and threw me under the bus. I told him that I did not ever want to speak to him again and not to ever call me again. We talked for a few more minutes, and the conversation ended with him hanging up in my ear. I was hurt, devastated, and in tears. I called a close friend and told her what went down, and she allowed me to cry on her shoulder. She was upset, yet happy that he was out of the picture. I, on the other hand, was broken.

See ... they thought you would curl up and let life pass you by. What they failed to realize is that you have an inner strength that will not allow you to give up or give in (1 John 4:4) ... Yes, the pain hurts, but the pain ... your hurt is preparing you for greater ... lift your HEAD UP! STEP ... STEP ... STEP ... KEEP MOVING FORWARD!

Chapter Seven
The Process

I was so hurt and angry. I could not believe what happened—how everything transpired. Are you kidding me? I cried, cried some more, and cried until I could not cry anymore. I felt like Levi plotted, schemed, and set everything up. I began to experience familiar feelings I felt in past relationships. I felt inadequate, weak, voiceless, powerless, and hurt. There was nothing I could do but take it. I was devastated.

The next morning I had an engagement, whereas I was scheduled to minister in dance. I really did not know how that would go, but I prayed and asked God to help me contain my tears. I was so broken. I've been broken before, but this time, I was completely shattered into many pieces. I felt so stupid ... so used. I felt like Levi completely deceived me. He painted a picture that was a lie. He pretended to want what I wanted and reeled me in, and then backed out when he knew he had me trapped. *What was I going to do? How was I going to get through this?*

Sunday morning I headed to church, and I was a mess. I cried the entire service. I felt so convicted in my spirit, ashamed, and hurt. When service was over, I remember calling my sister and sharing with her that I almost had sex with Levi, but I stopped it before it actually happened. She was in shock and could not believe what I was telling her. She had no idea I was so deep with him. Once I heard her reaction, I ended my conversation and tried to change the subject. I knew she would be shocked, but I had no idea she would react the way she did. I was afraid to share what all occurred in the few months that Levi and I were together so I kept it to myself. With all that I was feeling, I was still under the control of bondage. I covered it up by not exposing the truth of what I had done. I felt the disappointment in my sister's voice, and it was indescribable. I could not stop crying. I was a disaster, and I felt every bit of my broken heart, my shame, and guilt.

Monday morning came, and I headed to work. How was I going to get through the day? I had no idea! I thought it was ridiculous because the whole reason for me spending time with Levi was to get my attention off the issues that were occurring at my job. At this time, things began to be exposed at my job where I began to notice a great deal of deception. A specific picture was painted and promised to me, which was the main reason why I decided to accept the job—but that picture was a lie. Everything that happened since I graduated appeared to be deceitful, and the shattered pieces of my heart began to chip a little bit more. How did I get so caught up in this deception? I thought to myself, *What is going on, and how will I begin the healing process? Can I get over this?* It hurt so badly; I just wanted to hide and cry.

I remember calling a close friend and sharing with her that I felt the need to call Levi. I had so many questions, and I felt that things were not finished because he had hung up on me. She told me to do what I needed to do. I hung up the phone and called him. I was not surprised that he did not answer my call. As I began to leave a message, I noticed someone was calling me. It was him! I clicked over and began to speak with him. I shared that I was in the process of leaving a message, and needed to share some things with him. I said that I felt deceived. I felt like he planned the entire situation, which was messed up. I asked him if he ever cared about me and he said yes and that he still did. He shared with me that like me, he too was hurt and did not understand. I could not believe anything he said. I shared that I protected his feelings throughout our time together and the one and only time he needed to protect me, he tossed me aside. I began to cry and asked, "How could you paint such a picture that you knew you did not want and could not provide?" He asked me how I was feeling, and I told him, "BROKEN!" I was incredibly hurt, and he was the one who broke my heart. I said that he did what I feared would happen, and now I am left with my heart in pieces. We talked for about thirty minutes or so and then finally ended the conversation. He wanted to call me later that night, but I told him I still did not want him to call me ever again and that I did not want him attending my licensing ceremony. I made myself very clear that I was hurt and felt deceived.

Over the next couple of weeks, I had to prepare for my licensing ceremony. I went through bouts of depression, felt an immense deal of witchcraft around me, and battled mental warfare. I struggled with my self-esteem, self-worth, and confidence. I felt so unloved and so dirty that part of me wanted to call off the ceremony because I was not in a good place. I did not feel worthy of accepting the call; nevertheless, I fought my way through. I knew that if I called everything off, Satan would win. The whole situation was designed to kill me and stop me from walking into my destiny. I had to hold on and trust God. I had to stay strong somehow, some kind of way.

The morning of my licensing ceremony was peaceful. My sister and I went to the location early to make sure everything was set-up and in place. I was thrilled and anxious all at the same time. I had just gone through one of the toughest battles of my life, and here I was still willing to accept the call of ministry on my life but was not feeling worthy of such call. *What was I getting myself into?* I wondered, but I knew God would not put more on me than I could bear. I also knew I needed to go through with this because there were things God wanted me to do and this was part of His plan. The ceremony went well, and Levi respected my wishes of not coming. I was surprised that his mom did not show up. I just knew she would be there because she was so adamant about attending. When I dropped off the invitation at her house, she was so happy that I was accepting the call on my life and told me she would not miss my ceremony for anything. In any event, the day went well, and I was now a licensed ministry in the performing arts ministry. Things were beginning to look better, and I felt the love of God all over me; it was amazing!

A few days went by, and I received a text message from Levi's mom. She wanted to see how my ceremony went. She explained that she was out of town, but wanted to speak when she got back. I really did not know how to respond, so it took me a while. When I finally did, I texted the words to Tasha Cobbs' song "There is healing in the name of Jesus." I knew it threw her off, but I did not know what else to say. In the end, she told me that she would call me when she returned from her trip. I shared the text conversation with my sister and told her that I needed to speak with Levi's mom because I was not one for ignoring people. I like people to know how I feel and why I feel what I feel. I do not like playing games. So, I sought the face of God for strategy. I knew I needed to close every door that was connected to Levi, and his mother was the main connection.

Closing Doors

A few days went by, and I received a text message from Levi's mom. She told me she was back in town. I responded by asking her if she was free to meet up. We made plans for dinner later that night. I was a bit nervous because I had no idea how I would break the news of me needing to disconnect myself and cut off all communication with her. When the time came for us to meet, I texted her that I was on my way, and she asked if it was okay for her to ride with me. I responded that it would be fine. Again, I had no idea what would happen or how I would break the news. When I arrived, we hugged, and she was radiant. She had a beautiful smile on her face, and I was happy that we were hanging out. I really liked his mom, I enjoyed our talks, and time together; the limited time that we shared. We headed out, and we found ourselves at a nearby restaurant. We had a blast and a lovely dinner. I asked her about her trip, and she shared with much excitement how she enjoyed herself. One thing I have to say is that when we did talk, or when we hung out, we never talked about her son. There was one time when I asked her if she was okay with me dating her son being that I was seven years older. Other than that we never discussed Levi, so I had no idea how I would start a conversation about him. It just was not the nature of our relationship.

After dinner, we made a few stops, whereas she got the opportunity to ask me about dance. I shared a few things with her, and she wanted to know if I could train her because she had a desire to learn dance. I was a little hesitant to answer knowing I needed to disconnect but told her I would love to train her. As we continued to drive, I asked her if she talked to her son and she said yes. She said that he told her we broke up and that we were not on speaking terms. I agreed and told her that what he shared was correct. I asked her how she handled one of her relationship breakups, and she explained to me that she needed to cut everything off with the man. *Here is my time to explain my need for disconnection,* I thought. I told her I needed to cut everything off with her son and it starts with me disconnecting myself from everyone he was connected to and that included her. I told her I needed to do this because I could not have any door open that led to her son. She was shocked and said, "Are you breaking up with me?" I told her yes. I tried not to share too much with her because I did not want to provide too much information, but I did let her know that I was very hurt, and felt deceived. I felt like her son knew from the beginning he did not want what I wanted, but he continued to paint a picture that he did not want and never intended to produce. I told her he knew who I was before we both decided to go forward with our relationship. I asked him on numerous occasions if he was sure he wanted to pursue a relationship with me, but in the end, he did not want that. I also shared with her that I wish he would've been honest with me because had he been honest, we would've never gotten to this point. I would have never opened up to him. I would have ended it and walked away. She understood, and wanted to know if later she and I could be friends because she really liked me, but I told her no. The only way that would happen was if God touched my heart and I would be open to some kind of relationship with her son, but I did not foresee that. I told her I loved her son, and I really disliked how things ended between us, but it ended for a reason. She told me her son loved me too and then opened the door and got out of the car. I got out of the car as well, and we embraced and said our goodbyes.

He (Leviathan) beholds every high thing;
He is king over all the children of pride.
Job 41:34

Chapter Seven
I Heard About You

I thought over my whole life and the time I served in ministry. How many times have I placed myself in a pit, in a situation that I was never supposed to be in? I wondered ... *Have others been through similar situations, whereas they find themselves in a situation they knew they did not want to be in, but somehow when they looked up they were deeply involved?* I knew for me, I did not want to be in this situation, and hated what I created. I feel in love with the idea of someone ... I fell in love with someone's potential, and now I was left picking up the pieces of my broken heart. No matter how hard I tried to disconnect, I did not have the strength to leave or let it go. I did not have the will to walk away. I felt so much inside, but I embraced it. I cared so much for Levi that I pushed myself aside. I was in a trance. How did I get there? What was wrong with me? As I asked these questions over and over, I began to hear the word Leviathan. I've heard this word before, but could not remember where. I began to do research and located Leviathan in Job 41.

> Can you draw out Leviathan with a fishhook, or tie down his tongue with a rope? ²Can you put a cord through its nose or pierce its jaw with a hook? ³Will it keep begging you for mercy? Will it speak to you with gentle words? ⁴Will it make an agreement with you for you to take it as your slave for life? ⁵Can you make a pet of it like a bird or put it on a leash for young women in your house? ⁶Will traders barter for it? Will they divide it up among

the merchants? *7Can you fill its hide with harpoons or its head with fishing spears? 8If you lay a hand on it, you will remember the struggle and never do it again. 9Any hope of subduing it is false; the mere sight of it is overpowering. 10No one is fierce enough to rouse it. Who then is able to stand against me? 11Who has a claim against me that I must pay? Everything under heaven belongs to me. 12 I will not fail to speak of Leviathan's limbs, its strength, and its graceful form. 13Who can strip off its outer coat? Who can penetrate its double coat of armor? 14Who dares open the doors of its mouth ringed about with fearsome teeth? 15Its back has rows of shields tightly sealed together; 16each is close to the next*

that no air can pass between.
¹⁷They are joined fast to one
another; they cling together and
cannot be parted. ¹⁸Its snorting
throws out flashes of light; its eyes
are like the rays of dawn.
¹⁹Flames stream from its mouth;
sparks of fire shoot out. ²⁰Smoke
pours from its nostrils as from a
boiling pot over burning reeds.
²¹Its breath sets coal ablaze, and
flames dart from its mouth.
²²Strength resides in its neck;
dismay goes before it. ²³The folds
of its flesh are tightly joined; they
are firm and immovable. ²⁴Its
chest is hard as rock, hard as a
lower millstone. ²⁵When it rises up,
the mighty are terrified; they
retreat before its thrashing. ²⁶The
sword that reaches it has no
effect, nor does the spear or the

dart or the javelin. [27]Iron it treats like straw and bronze like rotten wood. [28]Arrows do not make it flee; sling stones are like but chaff to it. [29]A club seems to it but a piece of straw; it laughs at the rattling of the lance. [30]Its undersides are jagged potsherds, leaving a trail in the mud like a threshing-sledge. [31]It makes the depths churn like boiling caldron and stirs up the sea like a pot of ointment. [32]It leaves a glistening wake behind it; one would think the deep had white hair. [33]Nothing in earth is its equal-a creature without fear. [34]It looks down on all that are haughty; it is king over all that are proud. (Job 41 NIV)

A few days after I read this passage of scripture, Apostle John Eckhardt posted thorough information about the spirit of Leviathan, the king of pride. Apostle Eckhardt stated:

> *Leviathan, the spirit of pride, is mentioned five times in the word of God. Because the spirit of pride is common to mankind's fallen nature, it is a spirit that we all must battle. The book of Job says that once you begin to do battle with this particular spirit, it will be one of the most difficult battles you will ever have to fight. In our own strength, we are not able to destroy pride. If we are to be victorious, we must humble ourselves and let God deliver us from the spirit of Leviathan. (2014)*

In addition to this information, I remember reading a few books by Apostle Kimberly Daniels, in which she, too, thoroughly discussed the spirit of Leviathan. In her book "Clean House Strong House: A practical guide to understanding spiritual warfare, demonic strongholds, and deliverance," Apostle Daniels (2003) conveyed that:

> *Job 41:22 says, "Strength dwells in his neck." Pride and rebellion walk hand in hand. Rub your hands across the back of your neck. There is no flexibility in your neck. It is firm like a brick. God called Leviathan a "stiff-necked" spirit. When dealing with Leviathan, you must also deal with the demons that protect Leviathan (scales). The pride hides in the scales. Bind all the spirits that cover and garrison him, because Leviathan is the king of pride. These are the alliances of legions that cover up the real problem to protect the strongman. (pg. 37)*

Another book written by Apostle Daniels, "From a Mess to a Miracle," dedicated an entire chapter discussing the spirit of Leviathan. Apostle Daniels conveyed that Leviathan represents a strongman (To understand more about a strongman I recommend reading Dr. Cindy Trimm's Binding the Strongman).

Characteristics of Leviathan as discussed by Apostle Eckhardt and Apostle Daniels:

1. Leviathan creates a spirit of prayerlessness (Job 41:3a).

2. Leviathan speaks with harsh words (Job 41:3b).

3. Leviathan avoids servanthood (Job 41:4b) but loves to be served. This spirit thinks of itself more highly of itself and things of himself as King.

4. Leviathan rejects covenant (Job 41:4a).

5. Leviathan is stubborn and stiff-necked (Job 41:22) ... Stubbornness and rebellion are also manifestations of pride (Leviathan). Samuel 15:23 "rebellion is as iniquity and idolatry." This spirit makes people unstable.

6. Leviathan twists the truth. Isaiah 27:1 says, "In that day, the Lord with His severe sword, great and strong will punish Leviathan the fleeing serpent. Leviathan that twisted serpent;"

Apostle John Eckhardt stated that:

Individuals who are influenced by this spirit resist submission and walk around with a hardened heart. This spirit encourages individuals to break covenant (divine friendships, business partnerships, marriages, relatives, and leave churches). This spirit twists the truth around and is an expert in deception. This spirit wants to be in control and loves to play mind games by blinding individuals from truth. Individuals under its influence become delusional, critical, and judgmental. Individuals influenced by this spirit convey words of negativity that pull down others.

Finally, this spirit uses mockery to attack others. (2014)

For additional information on further reading, see Appendix A.

Settling ... that which you settle for requires much of you. And, in the end, you get hurt and experience great devastation.

Chapter Nine
Relatives

After researching the spirit of Leviathan, I began to ponder my situation. It was apparent I was somehow associated with and was influenced by this spirit, but for some reason, I felt like there was more. I began to revisit some situations with Levi, and I realized he mocked me often. He would repeat things I would say, but the way he would say them would make me feel small. He repeated things I said as if they were *his* beliefs and ideas. He camouflaged himself and played possum—reptiles camouflage themselves as a technique for survival. They mimic the background of the surrounding as a way to blend in so they will become overlooked or invisible. With this, I went back to the Leviathan spirit, and I decided to research

81

'mock.' I needed to understand how Leviathan related to what I was dealing with. I did a word search and found some interesting facts (see Table 1). The word search took me through a journey, which highlighted the bottom line of the situation with Levi.

Table 1

Word search on the word 'mock.'

Word search on the word 'mock.'	
Word	Definition
Mock	To mimic. Simulated.
Mimic	To imitate closely. To resemble by biological mimicry.
Mimicry	A superficial resemblance of one organism to another or to natural objects among which it lives that gives it an advantage (as protection from predation).
Simulated	To give or create the effect or appearance of: Imitate. Simulation.
Simulation	An object that is not genuine. The imitation by one system or process of the way in which another system or process works.
Imitation	To follow as a model. Copy. Resemble. Reproduce. Mimic. Counterfeit. Imitator.
Copy	Duplicate. Replica. An imitation or reproduction of an original work.
Resemble	To be like or similar to.
Reproduce	To produce again.
Counterfeit	Sham, spurious, forged. To copy or imitate in order to deceive. Pretend. Feign. Fraud, fake, imposture, deceit, deception.
Word search on the word 'mock' cont.	

Sham	Counterfeit, imitation, a person who shams. Pretends. Not genuine. False. Feigned.
Spurious	False, son of an unknown father. Not genuine. Eminence
Forged	A furnace or shop with its furnace where metal is heated and worked. To form (metal) by heating and hammering. Fashion, shape (an agreement). To make or imitate falsely with intent to defraud (a signature). To move ahead steadily but gradually.
Deceive	To cause to believe an untruth. To use or practice deceit. Beguile, betray, delude, mislead.
Deceit	Deception, trick, deceitfulness, dissimulation, duplicity, guile.
Deceitful	Practicing or tending to practice deceit. Misleading, deceptive.
Pretend	Feign, to lay claim.
Feign	To give a false appearance of. Sham. To assert as if true. Pretend.
Fraud	Deceit, trickery, trick. Imposter, cheat.
Fake	Counterfeit. Sham. Imitation, fraud, imposter. A simulated move in sports (as pretended pass). To deceive.

Word search on the word 'mock' cont.	
False	Not genuine. Artificial. Intentionally untrue. Adjusted or made so as to deceive (scales). Tending to mislead. Deceptive. Not faithful or loyal. Treacherous. Not essential or permanent. Inaccurate in pitch. Based on a mistaken ideal.
Falsehood	Lie. Absence of the truth or accuracy. The practice of lying.
Treacherous	Characterized by treachery. Untrustworthy, unreliable. Providing insecure footing or support. Traitorous, faithless, false, disloyal.
Treachery	Violation of allegiance or trust.
Traitorous	One who betrays another's trust or is false to an obligation. One who commits treason. To hand over, deliver, to betray.
Betray	To lead astray. Seduce. To deliver to an enemy. Abandon. To prove unfaithful to. To reveal unintentionally. Show, indicate, mislead, delude, beguile.
Delude	Mislead, deceive, trick.
Trick	To crafty procedure meant to deceive. A mischievous action. Prank. A childish action. A quick or artful way of getting results. Knack. Maneuver.

Word search on the word 'mock' cont.	
Maneuver	Planned and controlled movement or series of moves. Large scale exercise of troops, warships, etc. Often deceptive planned or controlled action. Skillful plan. Perform or cause to perform a maneuver. Handle adroitly. Stratagem, tactic, trick, gambit, subterfuge, ruse, dodge, exercise, war games, manipulate, run, drive, guide, navigate, steer, control, plot, scheme, machinate intrigue.
Stratagem	Cunning plan or scheme. Deceiving an enemy. Trickery.
Trickery	Deception. Monkey business.
Tactic	A plan action for accomplishing an end.
Gambit	An act of tripping someone. A chess opening in which a player risks once or more minor pieces to gain an advantage in position. A calculated move.
Artifice	Trick, trickery, an ingenious device; ingenuity.
Ingenuity	Skill or cleverness in planning or inventing: Inventiveness.
Inventiveness	Creative, ingenious. Characterized by invention (turn of mind).
Subterfuge	A trick or device used in order to conceal, escape, or evade. Fraud, Deception, Trickery.
Ruse	A wily subterfuge: trick, artifice.

Word search on the word 'mock' cont.	
Dodge	An act of evading by sudden bodily movement. An artful device to evade, deceive, or trick. Expedient. To evade by trickery. To move suddenly aside.
Expedient	Extricate, prepare, be useful. Adopted for achieving a particular end. Marked by concern with what is advantageous; governed by self-interest. A temporary means to an end.
Exercise	Employment, use. Exertion made for the sake of training or physical fitness. A task or problem done to develop skill. A public exhibition or ceremony. Exert, control. To train by or engage I exercise. Worry, distress.
Worry	To shake and mangle with the teeth. To make anxious or upset. To feel or express great care or anxiety: Fret. Trouble.
War Games	To be in conflict.
Manipulate	To treat or operate manually or mechanically with skill. To manage or use skillfully. To influence with intent to deceive.

Word search on the word 'mock' cont.	
Run	To take to flight. Flee. To go without restraint. To go rapidly or hurriedly. Hasten, rush. Operate. To continue in force. To flow rapidly or under pressure. Melt, fuse, and dissolve: discharge. To take in a certain direction.
Drive	To urge, push, or force onward. To carry through strongly. To direct the movement or course. Force, compel, to progress with strong momentum. To propel an object of play.
Guide	One who leads or directs another's course. One who shows and explains points of interest. Something that provides guiding information; signpost. A device to direct the motion of something. To act as a guide. Manage, direct.
Navigate	To sail on or through. To steer or direct the course of a ship or aircraft. Move
Steer	To direct the course.
Control	Directing influence over. Dominate.
Plot	A small area of ground. A secret scheme. To make a plan or contrive.
Scheme	A plan for doing something. A crafty plot. To form a plan.
Machinate	An act of planning to do harm. Plot.
Intrigue	Underhand Plot. Secret influence.

Word search on the word 'mock' cont.	
Adroitly	Secret scheme. A clandestine love affair. Plot.
Clandestine	Held in or conducted with secrecy.
Knack	A clever way of doing something. Natural aptitude.
Unintentionally	Not done by intention or design. Not intended.
Beguile	Deceived. To while away. To engage the interest of by guile.
Treason	The offense of attempting to overflow the government of one's country or of assisting its enemies in war.
Faithless	Disloyal, not to be relied on. False, traitorous, treacherous, unfaithful.
Disloyal	Lacking in loyalty.
Not Genuine	Not real, not authentic, not sincere, not honest.
Falsify	To prove to be false. To alert as so to deceive. Lie. Misrepresent.
Misrepresent	To represent falsely or unfairly.
Imposture	One that assumes an identity or title not one's own in order to deceive.
Deception	The act of deceiving. The fact or condition of being deceived. Fraud, trick.
Eminence	High rank or position. A person of high rank or attainment.
Fraudulent	Characterized by, based on, or done by fraud: deceitful.

As I went through each word, I could not believe I was open to such treatment. I could not believe the situation was clearly designed to harm and destroy me.

When it's all said and done ... forgive. Once you forgive, you are no longer under the control of that which hurt you.

Chapter Ten
Really

That awkward moment when I had to admit ... I got played. And, the hardest part to admit is that I helped him. I was so open and honest with him, and he used it to his advantage. I am not one for games, but I got played! My pride got the best of me for a while because I did not want to come to grips with the fact that a young guy played me and played me so well. He was skilled in playing the hurt guy role, and I fell for it. Although I knew some things were off and many things just did not add up, I sincerely wanted to believe that Levi was different. That he would not take who I was—an honest, genuine, and sincere person—and use it against me. I mean, everything I shared with him he turned on me and used it like it was a

91

weakness of mine. Maybe it was a weakness. Wanting to see the good in spite of the bad that I felt in my spirit, or wanting to truly believe that a person could not be so heartless and treat people like a box of tissue. It hurt, and again I was left wondering what was wrong with me.

Honestly, all the signs were there, I just did not want to believe that he was capable of such activity. I guess I believed that since he witnessed the hurt his mom went through, the hurt he endured in his relationships, and the fact I provided a safe environment for him, he would appreciate the person I was. That he'd appreciate the fact that I showed him the true me and that I was genuine—that I was what he said he never thought still existed. I wanted to believe him ... I did believe him and got hurt ... played ... and tossed aside like I did not matter ... as if I had no value ... and I almost believed the lie yet again! I literally helped this boy play me like an instrument. I helped him ... *I helped him.* In me focusing on just this aspect, I began to question my worth; I began to question whether or not I was a good woman. But, then I realized, he played a part in this as well. Yes, my role was huge, but wait—he had his place. He was a guy who played the role so well ...

His Characteristics

He has pride issues and fatherless issues. He uses others to get what he wants and then tosses them to the side as if he never knew them. He does what is needed to survive. He is a hunter (pursue, capture, and release). He pursues individuals to get what he believes he needs. He will lie, steal, and cheat just to get by in life; he is a survivor with the attitude of "by any means necessary." He uses people until he feels he is done with them. He is not used to people walking away from him because he usually controls and manipulates the situation so when he is done *he* walks, *he* releases the individual. He has made a habit of this. He had to, because this is what he does to survive. He feels like a failure because he has so many gifts and talents, but he ends up sabotaging opportunities because of his negative hunter's mentality. He hurt so many people that he is paranoid others are automatically out to hurt him. So, he gets them before they get him. He is a loner. One who carries great mystery about himself. He carries himself this way because he is an observer. He learns his prey and becomes his prey. He takes on the characteristics of those whom he hunts. He dislikes himself, and he targets those who appear to have great confidence, those who have strong self-esteem. Those with kind and gentle hearts. He never takes responsibility for his actions. He points the finger at everyone else and deceives himself into believing he is right, and the other person is wrong. He is full of anger ... full of hurt ... and full of pride. He is stuck in the bondage of needing to prove he is more than his past, but he continues to sow bad seeds because of that hunter mentality. He hates to lose, so he targets winners. He targets those who are—or appear to be—successful, and he tries to befriend them. He gives a sob story of how difficult his life is so they will feel sorry for him. This is how he traps his bait. He begins to share things with them to make them feel they are making a difference in his life only to reel them deeper into his web. He is a snake ... a cunning snake, and he is very clever. His voice is different, and his appearance is different. He is not the handsome or the fine type. He is just average. You second-guess yourself often because you cannot believe that this person could ever be so vile.

He baits individuals with a sob story and camouflages himself to blend in with the environment. He is a wannabe. He wants to be so much more than what he is but does not have the capability because of his nature. He was never taught or shown unconditional love so he does not know how to give or receive it. So, he lives life as a hunter and goes throughout life hunting others. He projects his insecurities, lack of self-worth, and lack of confidence on others. This is how he conquers his prey. This is a game to him, and he takes pride in the games that he plays. He is a cold-hearted snake. He is a man of words and is impressive with them. He uses words to bait his prey as well. But, he lacks the ability to display his words through action. He uses excuses to justify why he cannot move or act. His nature prevents him from doing this because he lacks the capacity to do so. He takes the words of his prey and twists them around. He is a master gaslighter. He turns things around to the point where you feel you are going crazy. He uses his craftiness until you are empty, or he believes you are empty. Once he makes the decision that you are empty, he releases you and leaves you for dead. There is no love in this person's heart. He is a mastermind deceiver and uses the weaknesses, or what appears to be weaknesses, to get what he wants.

"Refuse to be an option. You should be the choice."

Chapter Eleven
Why Me

I grew up in a sheltered environment. My parents never married and were in an off and on relationship until I was about seven years of age. I do not remember too much about my mom and dad's relationship, but I do remember a few things. I remember those times when my dad was in and out of my life and the times when he was around. I loved it. I was daddy's little girl and loved my daddy. He would take me with him to people's houses, and I would sit in the living room and watch television. I remember the time when my mom packed up all my dad's belongings, put them in a box and dropped them off at the junior college where he coached. I remember visiting my dad at work and practicing with his team.

Honestly, playing sports was my connection with my dad. He coached me and took me to my track meets and practices. I always wanted to make my daddy proud. I remember the times when my mom would wake me up late in the night telling me to get out of bed, that we had to leave because my dad was acting crazy. I remember my mom leaving home and going to Hawaii with one of her male friends. I remember spending a lot of time away from my mom. My mom worked long and hard for her family, which consisted of her and me. As she worked, I stayed with relatives, neighbors, and sometimes friends. Although I am the only child, I grew up around a lot of cousins, so I learned how to share and how to not like myself.

Throughout my childhood, I heard so much from so many people—Dyoni, I do not like people who do this and that ...

Dyoni, I need you to be this and that for me ... Dyoni, I need you to do this and that for or to such and such. Yes, things that should never happen to a child happened to me, and it opened doors of great perversion. I became whatever one person needed me to be, and I changed within seconds to be something completely different for the next person. I had no identity. My thinking was distorted, and what others may have thought was off or unacceptable, I did not find anything wrong with because I thought it was normal.

Manipulation was something that was always prevalent in my life. Everyone I knew used some form of manipulation to get whatever they wanted from me. It became so bad that I thought people who did not operate in manipulation were off and were the ones who had ill intentions. My idea of love was twisted. I witnessed so much and felt so much, but I could not convey any of it. I heard so much negativity about my dad and could not understand why someone would say such things to me regarding my dad. I grew up with a great deal of anger inside of me, but I never realized the anger within me was so tremendous until this situation with Levi occurred. I was forced to look at myself. Forced to take a deeper look at my family, my relatives, and how I was raised. I was a product of my environment and most—if not all—of my decisions were made based on perverted thinking.

Crazy thing, I cannot remember ever hearing my dad call me beautiful or say how proud he was of me. I only heard, "You can do this and that better." Such negativity. So, whenever someone highlighted something negative about me, I always thought they cared about me because they were taking out the time to tell me what I needed to change about myself to improve as a person. I became an overachiever. I needed approval from people, especially my mom. I so badly needed to spend time with my mom. I just wanted her time—I wanted to be with my mom, and I wanted my mom to want to be with me. Just me and her. Oftentimes, I felt like my mom chose others over me. I sometimes felt like my mom did not want to spend any time with me because I was just not good enough, so I overachieved, just to hear my mom say, "I am so proud of you." Although my mom *did* say she was proud of me, the lack of her spending time with me told me something completely different.

Things I learned about myself during this situation:

1. **Deeply hurt people, hurt people**

I knew I was a hurt individual, but I did not know to what extent. I realized I went out of my way to protect the feelings and hearts of others when in actually, I was preventing them from growing and learning. I was robbing them of any possibilities to mature. Unconsciously, I was the very poison that poisoned and tried to kill the very essence of my being.

2. **Extreme lack of self-worth**

Although I had excellent accolades and accomplished some wonderful things, I had no idea what I was worth. I had no idea of my value. I needed and wanted attention. I needed the opportunity to show how great I was, so I would *aggressively* go after those who were just as hurt, if not more. I attracted what I was, and I wanted to help them. I wanted to heal and change them. I had no standards, so I went with whatever and allowed everyone to treat me any kind of way because that's what I was used to. It was normal to do everything for someone, especially a man, because that's what I saw when it came to my dad. I saw women driving and doing everything for my dad, so I thought that I, too, needed to do that for a person I cared about—especially a man.

3. **People who love hard would do just about anything to see the good in others. We want to help.**

This is extremely dangerous and suicidal in so many ways because I would jeopardize my own wellbeing or safety for the well-being of others. I desperately wanted and needed love from a man that I would disregard all the warning signs that conveyed how dangerous the environment was. I was incredibly naïve in thinking that once people (man) saw how great I was, they would want to love me—they would want me. I would become whatever they needed of me, which literally robbed me of my identity. I willingly depreciated my value and self-worth without even knowing it. In the process of depreciating myself, I became this, that, and everything to everybody. I forgot who Dyoni was, but then again ... I never knew her. I was what people said I should be.

4. **False sense of security and confidence**

Arrogance is a false sense of confidence. Yes, I acted as if I had it all together, but I lacked confidence and security. My emotions were all over the place, and I allowed my emotions to control me in every way. I wore my emotions on my sleeve and on my face. I was so immature in that area. Although I was in my early 30's my emotions were stuck at 16. Thinking back, my first major heartbreak was at that age. I was emotionally devastated, and emotionally I remained—stagnant and childish.

5. **Disobedient**

I was extremely disobedient and found myself in many unwanted situations. When God told me to do something and do it a certain way, I would ask questions trying to figure out why. Instead of trusting God and believing He wanted the best for me, I questioned everything and learned the hard way. I was one who needed to see for myself after someone told me the stove was hot—so hardheaded. I was so adamant about doing things my way, what and how I thought they should be done. I halfway obeyed ...

just, disobedient.

6. **Unstable**

Because of all the changes I went through emotionally and spiritually, I was running from God, and I found myself unplanted. I did not have a church home where I fellowshipped. Although I had covering, I was not covered properly. I was so unstable in everything—my decision-making, my moods, my everyday lifestyle. I was a hot mess, but I learned how to cover it well. I was the queen of cover-up, and I learned from the best. I saw many people from friends, family, leaders, pastors—you name it! Trust me, I learned from the best.

7. **Prideful**

Pride is pride, no matter how small or how great. I was very prideful in so many areas of my life. Trying to do things on my own. Not allowing people to help me. Not being teachable and thinking I had things under control. Pride comes before a great fall, and I fell hard—right on my face! Even then, I wanted to fix it myself and deal with it. Just prideful!

I See You... You Cannot Hide!

How can the best of you ignite the best in a person ... but the best of the person ignites the worst of you? Unequally yoked!

Chapter Twelve
Relapse

Over the past few weeks, I began to have pain in the side of my stomach. It became so bad that I could not sleep. I remember feeling paranoid and thinking, *Oh my, did Levi give me an STD?* Although we did not have sexual intercourse, we had oral sex. STD's can be spread through oral sex, but there's only a small chance of that. But, based on my history, I am one who gets away with so little, so I just knew I needed to go to the doctor. With all of this going on in my mind—all the revelation and healing that I was receiving—I felt the intense need to call Levi to let him know what I was occuring and that he may need to get checked out too.

When I called him, I was so angry. I had no idea I was so angry with him still!

It had been two and a half months, and I was still angry as if everything had just happened. In our conversation, I shared with him what I was feeling, and hated the fact that I still cared when it was clear that he did not, but I wanted to stay true to my character. He said that yes, he would get tested, but he had no symptoms and had been tested a few years ago. I asked if he had had any sexual contact with anyone since he was last tested and he replied no, just me. From there he asked me how I was doing. "Are you kidding me?" I said. I am hurt and angry with you and how you did me. He said he understood why I felt the way I felt, but I needed to understand he truly loved me and still believed I was his wife. *This dude never quits!* I thought. My response to him was, "You say it, but when you have the opportunity to show it you fail to do so. Your actions tell me differently." I was harsh with him, and I had no intention of being so mean. Still, we talked for a while. I got so sick to my stomach that I ended up throwing up. It was insane! When I got back on the phone, I told him what happened, and he seemed to be very concerned. I told him I would keep him posted in regards to my doctor's appointment that I was scheduled within the next couple of days. He said okay and told me he would call me later. If I answered, I answered. If not, he would call until I answered.

Although I knew his nature, I actually wanted him to call me, and I anticipated his call. *What was that matter with me? Why am I still holding on thinking that he would be different?* He never called, and I was left angry yet again! I sent him a text that said:

Thank you. Thank you for reminding me that your actions silence your words. No need to call because your game, nor your call, is welcome.

I was so angry and hurt yet again. I felt so upset that I allowed my emotions to dictate my actions, and I ended up calling him. He did not answer, so I texted him and said this:

"I do not want to be angry with you anymore. I am tired. I called to apologize for lashing out at you yesterday and this morning. Although I feel exactly what I expressed, it does not give me the right to lash out, and for that, I apologize. I did not know I was still so angry with you. But, the fact of the matter is ... it really does not matter what was done, how it was done, or when it was done. In the end, someone got hurt ... we live, and we learn. That's what life is all about ... GROWTH!"

Then, I texted him a picture of a peanut butter cup, which was the nickname we called one another. I did not get a response from him, but for me, it was a way of releasing my anger and trying to move on from the feelings of wanting to hurt him back. I felt better, but that did not last long.

The next morning, I went for a run and could not stop crying. *Why was I so upset?* I broke down and called him. He answered the phone and was startled. He asked what was wrong and why was I crying. I told him that I hated the fact that I still loved him. He stopped me and said, "I still love you too. I did not want to share that with you because I felt like you tried to start some mess yesterday when you called me with the news that you shared." I told him, "I did not call to start a mess, I really called out of concern and I felt you needed to know what was going on with me and my body. I did not know I was still so mad until I heard your voice." He said that he was glad I called and wanted to share some things with me. He felt like he did not deserve me because he was hiding something from me and if I found out, he was afraid of losing me. I thought, *what could he possibly be hiding?* He said he was hiding that he smoked weed. I was shocked, but I acted as if I knew. I quickly responded by saying, "I knew you did something like that because I smelled it on you." I told him he was a grown man, and he should have told me. He said since he moved away, he had not smoked. From there, he said he was glad we had the conversation because we really needed to have that conversation. We talked for a little while longer, and he said he would send me some pictures, and I agreed to send him some as well. I also shared with him that the trust I had for him was broken, and we would have to work through some things in order to move forward from this. He agreed, and I felt a sense of ease. We hung up the phone, and I continued with my run.

Later in the day, I received a text with a few attachments from him. He looked really good, and I was happy about that. He mentioned a few things in regards to his external state. I was a bit hesitant because it was obvious his outer appearance changed, but the state of his internal appearance had yet to be seen. I told him I missed his face, but he did not respond to me. After a few hours, I sent him a picture of me, and he said that my smile meant a lot to him. I wanted him to prove it, and I asked him to define "a lot." He did not acknowledge my first comment but was quick to define *a lot*. He also was quick to tell me that my eyes looked a tad bit cold, and it looked like I was still carrying some things. I asked, "Carrying what?" He said, "You tell me?" I said, "Maybe it's the hurt you see." I then sent him an additional picture to observe, but he failed to acknowledge it.

Later in the day, I mentioned to my sister that I spoke to Levi and that it was tremendously interesting, but I was not honest with her regarding the entire conversation. I was still lying and trying to cover things up. I wanted so badly to tell her, but I knew she would have questions, so I tried to keep it short. But, I knew I was not fooling her. It was only a matter of time until things would hit the fan. I just knew it, because I hated how I felt.

The next day, I was in so much pain I knew I needed to go to the doctor. I ended up going to Urgent Care to get some things checked out. I called Levi to inform him of this, and he acted awfully concerned. We talked, and he shared some things with me. By the time I checked in and sat down, I was called in to see the doctor. I took numerous tests. I sent a text to my sister to let her know I had to go to Urgent Care because my side was hurting so badly. I tried to let her know I was okay, and I would keep her informed of everything. My appointment went well, and the doctor said if there were any concerns, he would call to consult with me. I was a bit frightened because I had no idea what was happening to me.

Later in the day, I remember something that was said ... I needed to fortify my walls. I needed to protect myself. This came from the mouth of the one whom I was struggling to get free from. Levi had a point, it wasn't that I did not know this; it was just hard because I had already opened myself up to him and I was having a hard time believing how things were really going down between us. I remember texting him and telling him that:

> *When you want something ...*
> *there is a price that must be paid,*
> *whether small or large. When you*
> *desire something more precious*
> *than a red ruby ... there is a great*
> *price to pay. You see, red rubies*
> *are rare. One must go above and*
> *beyond the call of duty just to put*
> *a down payment for this rare gem.*
> *If you believe the makings of this*
> *rare ruby is your dream come true,*
> *then you must be willing to count*
> *the cost. Walls up. Can you afford*
> *the price?*

He did not respond to it, which was a little frustrating, but it was what it was. I was setting things up to test the spirit, something that I failed to do at the beginning of our relationship.

Unfortunately, I needed more information to understand that Levi was just not for me. Crazy, right? What else did I need to find out? So, yes, I placed myself in the line of fire yet again hoping that things would be different. We talked throughout the day, and I had many questions, but nothing alarming that would make me say *you do not deserve me.* I mean, we all fall short, and no one really deserves anything because of our sinful nature. These were the thoughts in my head to justify my reasons for trying to work things out with him. I loved him, and I really wanted things to work out. I wanted things to get better, and I was sure he wanted the same thing. He told me he did and said he was willing to prove it and show me.

At some point in time, you must ask yourself, "Is this PURPOSE or a DISTRACTION? 'This' could be a person, a job, a situation, or a habit ... Is this part of my purpose or is this distracting me from my purpose?"

Chapter Thirteen

Brokenness is My Middle Name

I had a dream early the next morning, and the dream startled me. I dreamt that I was in an unfamiliar place. I was driving in a car, and there was only one car on the road with me. We were both parked at a stoplight and out of nowhere, I noticed a change in the weather. It appeared that a huge tornado was about to occur, but I had nowhere to go. I knew I had to endure it and hope to God to make it through. Once I thought this, the car behind me flew into the air and then my car flew too. All of a sudden, there was a bright light, and I was walking on the street where I was parked. I asked people if they knew me, but they had no idea who I was. These were people that I had some form of relationship with. They were not close friends or family, but they were people that knew me or knew of me. The odd thing was that I gave them a different name. I told them my name was Dana. They told me Dana died in a crazy tornado. But, it freaked me out because I thought I *was* Dana.

When I woke up, I texted a friend of mine. I asked her if she had a dream about me and if so what was the dream about? She told me she had not dreamt about me. She then wanted to talk, so I told her I would call her later. I then called Levi to speak with him. He answered the phone, and I began to ask him questions. I needed to know who he smoked weed with. I needed to know if he was willing to give it up and stop completely. He told me he smoked with someone close to him and that it was something they did to bond. He said it was only something he did on occasions. It was not an addiction, and he could stop whenever he wanted. He said he would stop once he put the ring on my finger. I was floored. "Are you kidding me?" I said. "Stop now!" He then went into this spiel saying, "At least I do not drink until I get drunk." I was a little confused because I had a glass of wine here and there, but I was never irresponsible with it. I never got drunk, so I had no idea why he would say such things to me. I began to get angry all over again! I told him, "When you love someone, you are willing to sacrifice, you are willing to do what is needed to make it work. You are willing to give of yourself." I told him, "I sacrificed a lot for you because I wanted to. I sacrificed because I cared for you. I sacrificed my time, and I even sacrificed relationships." He said, "I never asked you to." The anger that I felt! He said, "You called me asking questions. I am not going to stop. I do not have a problem, and besides, I do not feel any conviction from God about it." He felt like it did not mess with his finances, so he was cool with it. I said to him that smoking weed was so much more than just smoking; it opened the door for other things which could be bad. He said, "See, this is why I did not want to tell you. I knew this would happen." I responded by saying, "And, you do not feel this is wrong. I mean, you felt you needed to hide this from me so it must be something that you felt was wrong." I asked him to please stop, and he said, "No, I will not. I will not, and that is that." In complete shock, I told him I was not settling for this. I compromised on a lot of things for this relationship, but this is where it ended. Then I hung up. I then called back, he answered, and I said, "Just to be clear, it is over. We are done." He said, "I figured as much." He made me so angry. I was furious! I told him he hurt me yet again, and enough was enough. Then, the conversation ended. Once I got off the phone, I cried and cried and cried. I could not believe this was happening yet again, but this time, I did it to myself. I knew—I just did not want to believe—that he was so cruel and deceitful.

Once I got myself together, I called a friend of mine, and we talked. I shared my dream with her. I also shared my conversation with Levi although she had no idea of the history we had. She said I needed to leave him alone and that it was his loss. I stated that I knew that, but why was it so hard for me to walk away and let go? She shared a few additional things with me, and we ended our conversation.

"Even in your brokenness, you are useful."

Chapter Fourteen
Enough is Enough

That night, I had a difficult time sleeping. I wanted so badly to call Levi, but I just did not have the strength to do it. I was so tired of being the one to reason and try to make things right. I wanted this to be over. Eventually, I cried myself to sleep, after reflecting on how I allowed him to get me so upset and to act outside of my character. The next morning, I had a difficult time getting out of bed, but I forced myself to get up and get going. I had a few meetings, so I had to get it together.

I was doing well despite the events that just took place. I was hurt, but I knew I needed to stay focused. I needed to focus on my business, focus on what needed to be purged from my heart, and

126

purged from my soul. As I pondered on needing to be purged, I received a text message from Levi. He was extremely malicious. He sent me a quote, and it pissed me off. He said that he hoped I had learned from my mistake of trying to prove a point so I will not make the same mistake in my next encounter. There were so many things I wanted to say to him—I was heated! I ended up sending him a video about smoking weed. Of course, I did not hear a response from him. I called him, and of course, he did not answer. I then texted him and told him that I was not calling to fight or argue. After a few minutes, I called him again, and he finally answered. I shared with him that it was not about me proving a point. He said he was tired of me pointing out how consistent he was in his inconsistencies. He said it, not me. All I wanted was for him to show his love for me and not just say he loved me. He stated that I was killing him, and he was tired of me repeating myself. I thought to myself, *Wow, this dude!* He went into his explanation of how busy he was with his new job and that he just needed to let me go and then he hung up. Wow, this was so familiar! The entire scene just played out the same way of my initial hurt. It took me a while to realize what he said, and once I came to myself, I sent him a text:

> *"Wow. You never had me back. Test the spirit by its fruit. Your fruit is foul. REPENT!"*

The Root

I was so angry! By this time, my sister wanted to know everything that transpired and I shared with her. She was so upset and mentioned that everything started with her, and it needed to end with her.

She explained that she would talk about me to him and since the first time he met me, he plotted to get me. She asked me to call him and I did. I called him, and I gave her the phone. I did not think he would answer, but he did. She spoke to him and told him not to contact me anymore. That if he wanted to talk to me, he needed to go through her first—that since all of this started with her, it was going to end with her. He said he was in a conference at the time so he would have to call her back. She said it was no problem and gave him her phone number and email and ended the call.

Once she got off the phone, she told me that in order for this to be conquered we needed to work together. This thing tried to divide us so it could conquer me and that we had to stick together. Again, I went through major mind games and battled all night with crazy thoughts.

Coming Clean

Later, when my sister got off work, she told me that she had battled with mind games! I shared that I had also battled them. She asked me some questions, and I spilled all of the beans. I told her that I called Levi first. She said, "But I thought you said he called you?" I shared that I initially called him and then he called to ask me how I was doing. I was tired of lying and trying to cover everything up, so I told her everything. I told her that I called him because I needed to share some information with him. She asked what information. I told her that I was experiencing some issues with my body and I needed to let him know that he needed to get checked out. I shared that all the test came back negative and the doctor said nothing was wrong with me.

She asked what I meant, and I told her that although I did not have intercourse with him, we did have oral sex. She was shocked. She said, "Why didn't you share this with me when you first told me you almost had sex?" I told her that I heard how she reacted when last I shared, so I did not provide additional information. She said, "Well, then, everything makes sense. This is why it is so hard for you to let this go—you connected yourself to him!" She said, "This is your opportunity to get free. What else happened?" I spilled it all—my morning visits with him, our conversations in the morning, throughout the day, and night. I told her everything! It was difficult because I knew what I had to say would disappoint her because I kept all of this from her by being so secretive. I told her that I did not share this information with her or anybody else because I knew how everyone felt about him. It was difficult talking about him, so I kept everything to myself. I told her I confessed everything to God already, so I did not have any unconfessed sin. We talked for a while and in the end, she said that God was not going to let me get away with what I did. I committed a sin and then tried to cover it. She was right, and I could not argue with her.

Usually, I share everything with my sister because we hold one another accountable for our actions, but I just did not want to disappoint her by sharing all that I had done. Because I was so secretive about my relationship with Levi, I fell deeper and deeper into sin. She asked me if I shared everything and other sins began to come to mind ... sins that I committed years ago that I never confessed to anyone ... sins that I forgot I had committed. It was a wild night! I shared with her things I never imagined I would share with anyone, and it felt liberating to get such things off me. Once I finished, she said, "Okay, we have to fight this thing together. We *have* to stick together. It tried to divide us to conquer and destroy you, so we have to come together to conquer this." I agreed with her and agreed that I would not hide anything else concerning this situation.

Conviction

Later that night, I went to bed and had a hard time sleeping. I was still being tormented in my mind about having oral sex with Levi. I could not understand why, because I confessed everything—but I failed to confess *how many* times I engaged in oral sex with him. I decided to get up and call my sister to share with her that I engaged in the activity twice, and it went both ways—I gave, and I received. It was difficult sharing this, but I needed to get completely free. She asked me if I had more to share and I said no, that I was really finished this time. We both went back to sleep.

A few hours went by, and I felt so dirty ... I cried, decided to call my sister again, and she consoled me. She told me that I became one flesh with him because of my actions. I did not think of it that way because I did not have intercourse with him, but I was sexually intimate with him, and should not have engaged in such activity outside of marriage. I told her that now I suffer with my self-worth and self-esteem. She asked me if she could ask me a question and I said of course. She asked me about a man that I met in Atlanta and if I did anything with him. I told her no. Normally, I would take offense, but I understood why she would ask me such question. I lied, covered up, and downplayed so much that when it concerned Levi, she wanted to make sure I did not do the same thing with a different guy a few years back. She shared some things with me concerning her past, and we talked. It felt good, but it hurt all at the same time because I betrayed her trust by not being honest. I did not know what would happen with our relationship because of this. We continued to talk, and I asked her if Levi called her and she said no. I told her to call him, and she did. As was usual, he did not answer.

Turning Point

We started getting ready for church, and I was looking forward to the message that day. The message was about wandering in the wilderness. I was so full that I cried almost the entire service. At the end of the service, the pastor provided an invitation to be baptized. I did not hesitate! I jumped out of my seat and walked down to the altar. I wanted to be free! I wanted to be rebuilt. I wanted to start fresh. It was my way of saying *God, I messed up, I need forgiveness; I surrender to your will.* I was making a declaration with my actions. Although I had been baptized before, this time felt different for a number of reasons: (1) it was unplanned, (2) I confessed every sin—sin that God brought back to my attention before this moment, and (3) I felt so ashamed and wanted to hide. Satan fought me and tried to make me miss my opportunity to get washed and made new. As soon as I changed my clothes and waited to enter the water, I cried more tears ... tears of repentance ... tears of joy ... knowing that I did not have to remain in the state that I had remained in for so many years. I was so angry and had so much anger in my heart. I was angry with my life, angry with the hurt I felt in my heart, and angry with people that hurt me.

When I was finally immersed in the water, I felt the love of God all over me. I felt renewed and forgiven. I was overwhelmed with tears of joy.

ENDURE the process ... I guarantee you will never be the same. STAND STRONG!

Chapter Fifteen
Goodbye

The next day, I felt lighter. I felt the new direction in which God was directing me. It felt so good, but I knew there were some things that I needed to do. I still needed to close the final doors with Levi. I realized I still had a poem from him that I needed to get rid of. I did not know whether I wanted to burn it or just throw it in the trash. I decided to do neither. I needed to make it clear that I was done, so I put the poem in an envelope and decided to leave it on his mom's car. I waited a few days before I solidified the action plan. I needed to make sure this was what God wanted and not something just to get a reaction from Levi. When I finally decided to get rid of the poem, I began to feel overwhelming anxiety; my heart began to flutter as if I was about to go to battle. So, I had my sister go with me. As we drove, I felt fear come upon me. It was crazy! Once I let the poem go, I felt yet another level of liberty. Nevertheless, I felt there would be some type of retaliation, so I prepared myself.

Revelation

A day went by, and I began to finally fight the mind games. I began to have thoughts of calling Levi. I began to revisit our relationship, and I found myself getting depressed. I had to fight and war against depression because it would come and go. I continued battling with my self-esteem, self-worth, and confidence. I realized those were some of the things that were under attack. Levi wanted what I had because he lacked them. I received the revelation that he was operating in my stuff—my self-esteem, my self-worth, my confidence—

and I wanted it back! He walked away from me taking so much and leaving all his mess for me to deal with. I had to war in the spirit and take back my stuff. In the process of me warring in the spirit, I felt the need to research. I found one of his ex-girlfriend's sites and found his Instagram information. As I surfed the page, I realized Levi was a pathological liar. Everything that came out of his mouth was a lie! The person he portrayed himself to be on his page was someone completely different from the person I knew. I found many interesting things that saddened me and made me angry and hurt all at the same time. This is what God was trying to protect me from. With his Instagram page and what I knew of him, he appeared to be a sociopath. I was shocked. In addition, I realized he monitored some of *my* social media sites. It freaked me out, but again he was strategic. He was a mastermind at playing games, and he knew how to get a reaction from me. In finding out about his frequent visits to my sites, I decided to block him and some of his close friends from viewing my sites. It was insane that I needed to do this. It was also insane because I began to view his page once a day and the sad thing was, every time I saw that page, I would get my feelings hurt because I would realize who he really was. I was tricked. Although I knew this, it was difficult actually seeing it plain as day. I tried to stop viewing his page, but it was as if I was in a trance—as if I was being controlled by him.

I then stumbled onto a YouTube video regarding breakups. The video discussed ways to get over a breakup. *Really, did I need to hear this?* I tried to close the video, but it would not close. It continued to play, and I ended up hearing the six steps of getting over a breakup: (1)

feel the pain, (2) put away and get rid of everything that reminds you of your ex, (3) do not call or text your ex, (4) stay away from the internet ... do not stalk your ex on social media sites. *Wow!* (5) stay around positive people, people who will get you to do positive activities, and (6) seek out help if needed. I was stunned! After that video, I vowed to stay away from his social media site and redirect my focus. God delivered me, and now it was my job to maintain my deliverance.

I continued to battle depression, but I knew that God was with me and that I had the victory. I began to realize my value, and I began to smile again. I began to live—and started to love myself again. I had some easy days and some difficult days, but God always reminded me that I was not alone. Knowing that God was with me, that numerous people loved me and had my back in prayer and support, I no longer felt empty. God reminded me that goodness and mercy were with me and that he refined my gifts and talents making them so much better than the former. I was in a new season, and this new season looked so bright!

It's a new season ... it's a new season. Old things must be left behind. Don't be afraid to let go ... release it ... leave it behind. Only you know what your IT is. Choose this day to move forward and not look back.

Conclusion

After going through this situation, I had to figure out why I was open to this form of hurt. Why did I have to experience and go through such pain? What was in me to attract such a character? In order for me to get it—to completely get the lesson that I needed to learn—I had to get to the root of my stuff. I had to investigate these questions.

Once I began to investigate these questions, I began to see things and recognize patterns. I recognized that I allowed many people—both men and women—to treat me any kind of way. Why was this? Why did I allow people to treat me as if I had no value and little self-worth? Because, the fact of the matter was, I did not think very highly of myself. People only mimicked the treatment I afforded to myself. I teach people how to treat me. I teach people how to speak to me. It was *me*. I was the one!

Once I understood this hurtful reality, I had to come to grips with how I felt about this. It was not easy accepting this, but I had to be brutally honest with myself, and I needed to deal with the inner hurt of my heart. See, I was in such a place of despondency. A place where life lived *me* and I went along with whatever and whomever. I lived in a vicious cycle where I jumped out of one prison only to find myself in another prison that was more severe and life threatening. I connected to people who had major issues because I had major issues. I was a dead girl walking with layers on top of layers that needed to be dealt with, and I needed to deal with each layer one at a time. As I dealt with each layer one at a time, I realized they were all connected in one way or another. But, I was the one who pushed stuff under the table. I was the one who allowed things to go on without addressing anything. I never knew how broken and bruised I was until I stopped all the busy work and made time to process how I felt about things ... about my stuff. I realized that the root of my stuff had nothing to do with me— *absolutely nothing to do with me.* I was wrestling with something that did not belong to me. It was something that was projected upon me, and I willingly accepted it as my own ... and I did this unconsciously. This is what happens when we do not take the time to process our stuff and examine ourselves. We end up living life carrying other people's stuff thinking it's our own, and we allow such stuff to determine our movements and our behavior.

See, my foundation was rocky. I never had a solid foundation. I never really knew who Dyoni was, so I became this and that for everyone, which opened the door to all kinds of things at such a young age. For me, age three was the time that I began carrying other people's stuff. This was the time that I was required by someone to perform sexual activities with a cousin of mine. I was not forced, but rather told we were going to play a game, so it was not placed upon me as something bad ... we were just playing a game. From there, we played other games that were clearly not appropriate for a three or four-year-old child. But, I never felt the huge desire to tell or share with anyone because it was never said—*YOU BETTER NOT TELL ANYONE!* The manipulation was subtle and to the natural eye, it did not look like manipulation. I had to deal with all of this.

I had to come to grips that it was not me, but rather the other individuals. I had to understand that it was not an issue that I had, but it was an issue the individual had that was projected onto me. For a long period of time, many things I did was a manifestation of the shame that was placed upon me. Everything I did or did not do was a result of someone else's stuff that I was forced to harbor and deal with—and I had no idea.

I went through a process where I had to forgive myself and others. I needed to let go, let go, and let go over and over again. This was so difficult because, throughout the process, I would see and recognize so much. I would cry and withdraw and become angry, but I needed to allow myself to feel this—I needed to touch my pain and identify with it. In doing so, I was able to forgive myself of the shame and guilt I lived with almost all my life. I was able to see those who were involved in different situations throughout my life from a different perspective. *Could it be just as they projected their stuff upon me others did the same to them?*

This question helped me become empathetic and compassionate of others because they had no way of knowing how not to repeat the pattern. Understand, I am not justifying anyone's actions, and I am not placing blame on anyone either. I am owning up to my part and yet acknowledging the role of others. I may not ever understand why others do what they do even if I asked, but I am responsible for me and how I respond, react, or lack thereof. Everything I do, I am held accountable for, not other people. I needed to get to the root of my stuff for me. I wanted to get free from my stuff. I no longer wanted to be controlled by my past or others.

That desire lit a fire under my butt to address and process my stuff. The root was found, and it was found once I made the decision to uncover my truth and talk about it no matter how it made me look or feel. Once I exposed myself and the part I played, I was able to see the entire picture, which led me to the root. The root is now uncovered and can no longer hide. I SEE IT and IT CAN NO LONGER HIDE. It cannot manipulate or control my life anymore. It cannot hide behind the manifestations of my actions portraying to be one thing when it's something completely different. I see it, and I am finally aware of all the tactics and patterns. I am better equipped to counteract with constructive and intentional positive activity that will continue to expose the root instead of counteracting with negative moments to cover up the root by throwing dirt on it.

Today, I encourage you to research yourself. Do an investigation and deal with some areas of your life. Deal with the hurt within your heart. Once you identify the root, you will no longer be controlled by it. You will be able to address it, deal with it, uproot it, and freely live. Live out the destiny and purpose God predestined for you and only you.

Remember, we are all works in progress, and we all have our starting point. We are all individuals, and we deal with things differently, and that is okay! I hope my truth encourages you to take the necessary steps to address some things, process them, and deal with them in a positive manner. You deserve to walk in liberty ... to live free from the hurt of the past whether imposed by others or placed upon yourself.

Dr. Dyoni Cole

Please pray with me ...

Father God, I give you all of me. I surrender myself to you, and I open myself to you and your healing power. I understand that this process will not be an easy one, but I trust you. I trust that your plans for my life are good and not evil. I believe you are a God of love, and I know you love me with an everlasting love. I believe you desire for me to be whole and complete in you. I believe you want the best for me. I am broken and bruised, and I need you, Lord, to touch every aspect of my heart. My heart hurts, and I want to be free. I desire to be free. This desire that I have to be free comes from you, and I receive it. Have your way in me ... in my heart. Teach me how to process things in a healthy manner. Teach me how to value myself the way you value me. You valued me so much that you sent your son to die for me. You gave the life of your only begotten son to die, so I may live and live freely. Forgive me Father God for all my sin. Forgive me Father God for not trusting you. Forgive me Father God for trying to live life according to how I thought to live. I surrender my all to you. Here I am. I give you permission to heal my heart. I give you permission to teach me how to love myself. I give you permission to cleanse me from inside out. Do a complete transformation in my heart. I believe you are the God who heals.

In Jesus' Name,
Amen.

After all the hurt ... disappointments ... sabotage ... plots ... schemes ... and deceit ... you are still here. That stuff was designed to destroy you, but it developed ... maturated your character... and strengthened you. Continue to STAND STRONG! God is with you, and will finish the work He started within you!

References

Abate, F. (1997). The Oxford: Desk Dictionary and Thesaurus (American Edition)
New York: Berkley Books

Apostle John Eckhardt (2014), The Spirit of Leviathan
Received from Apostle John Eckhardt's Facebook page.

Daniels, K. (2002). From a Mess to a Miracle
Lake Mary, FL: Creation Publishing

Daniels, K. (2003). Clean House Strong House: A Practical Guide to Understanding Spiritual Warfare, Demonic Strongholds, and Deliverance
Lake Mary, FL: Charisma Media

Harris. T. (n.d). How Animal Camouflage
Works
Retrieved from
www.science.howstuffworks.com/zoology/
all-about-animals/animals-
camouflage1.htm

Life Application Study Bible(2004), New
International Version
Wheaton, IL: Tyndale House Publishing,
Inc.
Grand Rapids, MI: Zondervan Publishing
House

Appendix A

Recommended Books

Daniels, K. (2005). Delivered to Destiny
Lake Mary, FL: Charisma Media

Larry, R. (2008) From the Guttermost to
the Uttermost
Bloomington, IN: Xlibris

Elkhart, J. (2014). God's Covenant With
You for Deliverance and Freedom: Come
Into Agreement With Him and Unlock His
Power
Lake Mary, FL: Charisma House

Trimm, N. C. (2005). The Rules of
Engagement Volume 1: The Art of
Strategic Prayer and Spiritual Warfare

Lake Mary, FL: Creation Publishing

Trimm, N. C. (2006). The Rules of
Engagement: Binding the Strongman
(Volume Two)
Lake Mary, FL: Creation Publishing

Trimm, N.C. (2010). The Art of War for
Spiritual Battle: Essential Tactics and
Strategies for Spiritual Warfare
Lake Mary, FL: Charisma House

I See You... You Cannot Hide!

Other Books By

Dr. Dyoni D. Cole

4 Steps to Deal with Your Issues
(September 2016)
Dance Leadership: Conflict Resolution
(TBA)
Fragments of My Heart (TBA)
Beautiful Tears (TBA)
The Journey of God's Dancer: A Daily
Devotional (TBA)

~Academic Books
Mr. Dissertation (TBA)

~Books for Children
Mommy Loves You (TBA)
Daddy Loves You (TBA)

Dr. Dyoni Cole

Made in the USA
San Bernardino, CA
27 September 2016